I0814251

Best Inventions

Automobile

by Julie Murray

Dash!
LEVELED READERS
An Imprint of Abdo Zoom • abdobooks.com

Level 1 – Beginning
Short and simple sentences with familiar words or patterns for children who are beginning to understand how letters and sounds go together.

Level 2 – Emerging
Longer words and sentences with more complex language patterns for readers who are practicing common words and letter sounds.

Level 3 – Transitional
More developed language and vocabulary for readers who are becoming more independent.

abdobooks.com

Published by Abdo Zoom, a division of ABDO, PO Box 398166, Minneapolis, Minnesota 55439.
Copyright © 2023 by Abdo Consulting Group, Inc. International copyrights reserved in all countries. No part of this book may be reproduced in any form without written permission from the publisher. Dash!™ is a trademark and logo of Abdo Zoom.

Printed in the United States of America, North Mankato, Minnesota.
102022
012023

Photo Credits: Getty Images, Granger Collection, Shutterstock
Production Contributors: Kenny Abdo, Jennie Forsberg, Grace Hansen, John Hansen
Design Contributors: Candice Keimig, Neil Klinepier, Colleen McLaren

Library of Congress Control Number: 2022937315

Publisher's Cataloging in Publication Data

Names: Murray, Julie, author.
Title: Automobile / by Julie Murray
Description: Minneapolis, Minnesota : Abdo Zoom, 2023 | Series: Best inventions | Includes online resources and index.
Identifiers: ISBN 9781098280161 (lib. bdg.) | ISBN 9781098280697 (ebook) | ISBN 9781098280994 (Read-to-Me ebook)
Subjects: LCSH: Automobiles--History--Juvenile literature. | Inventions--Juvenile literature. | Cars (Automobiles)--Juvenile literature. | Inventions--History--Juvenile literature.
Classification: DDC 629.22209--dc23

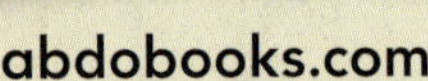

Table of Contents

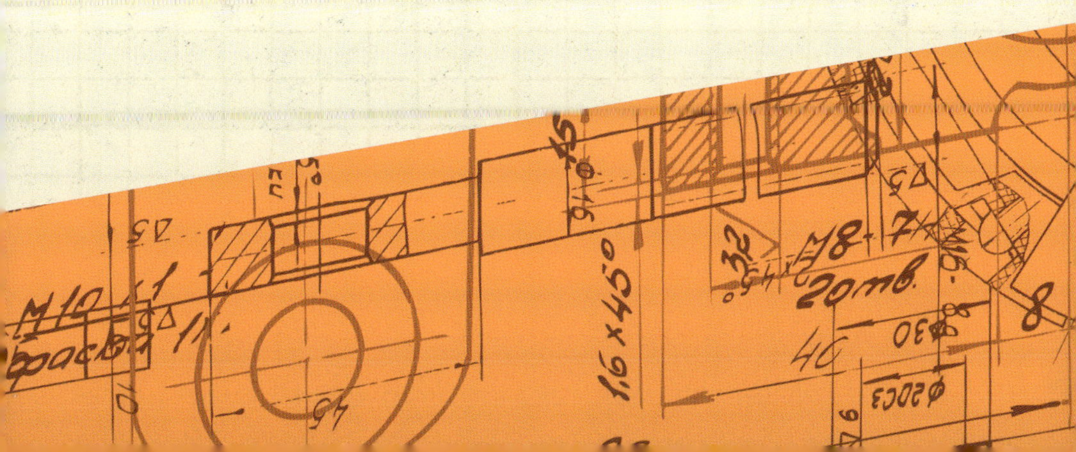

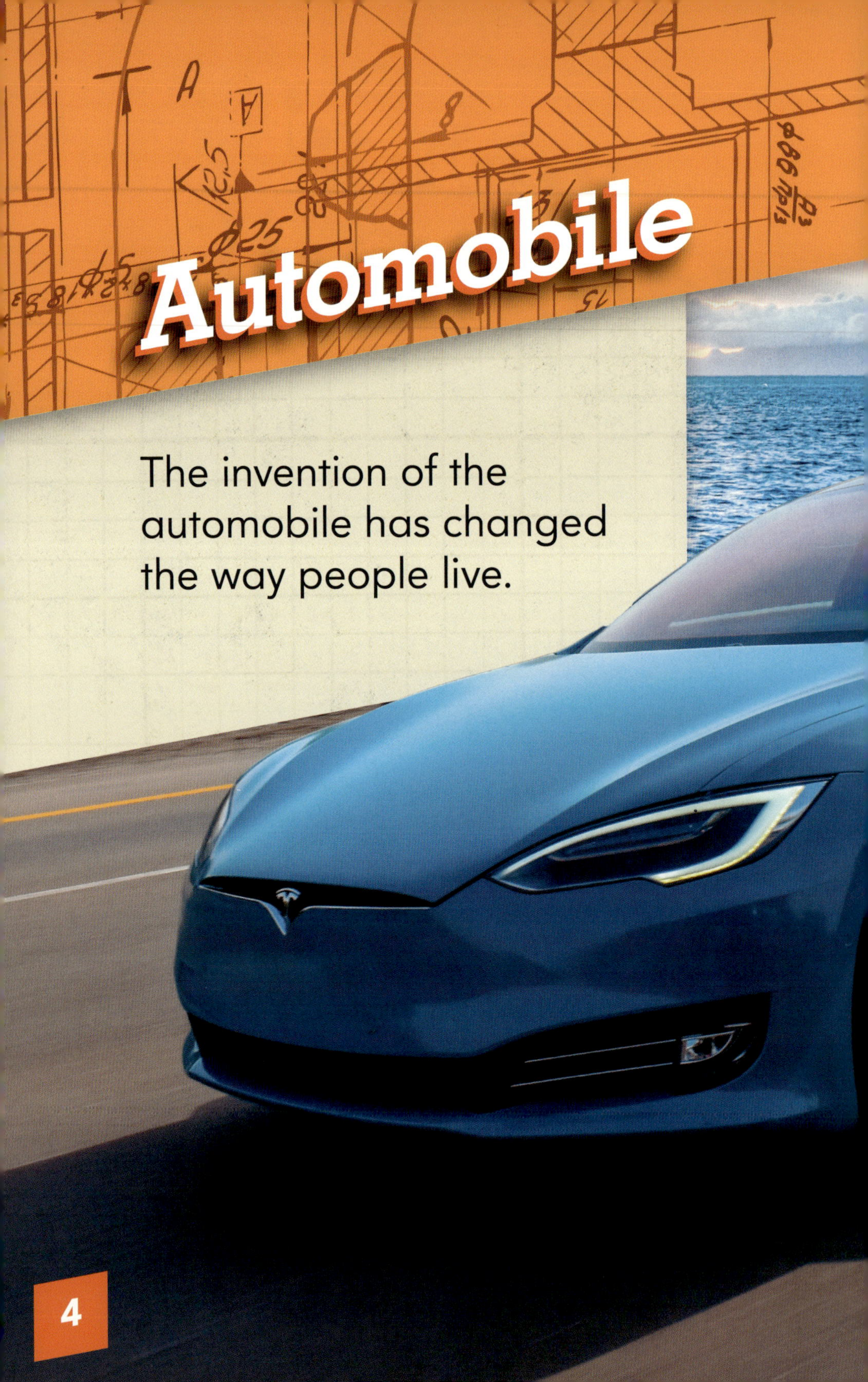

Automobile

The invention of the automobile has changed the way people live.

From driving to work to traveling long distances, automobiles get us from one place to another.

An automobile is often called a car. It has four wheels. It is powered by an engine and is mainly used to transport people.

M3
G384 CUK

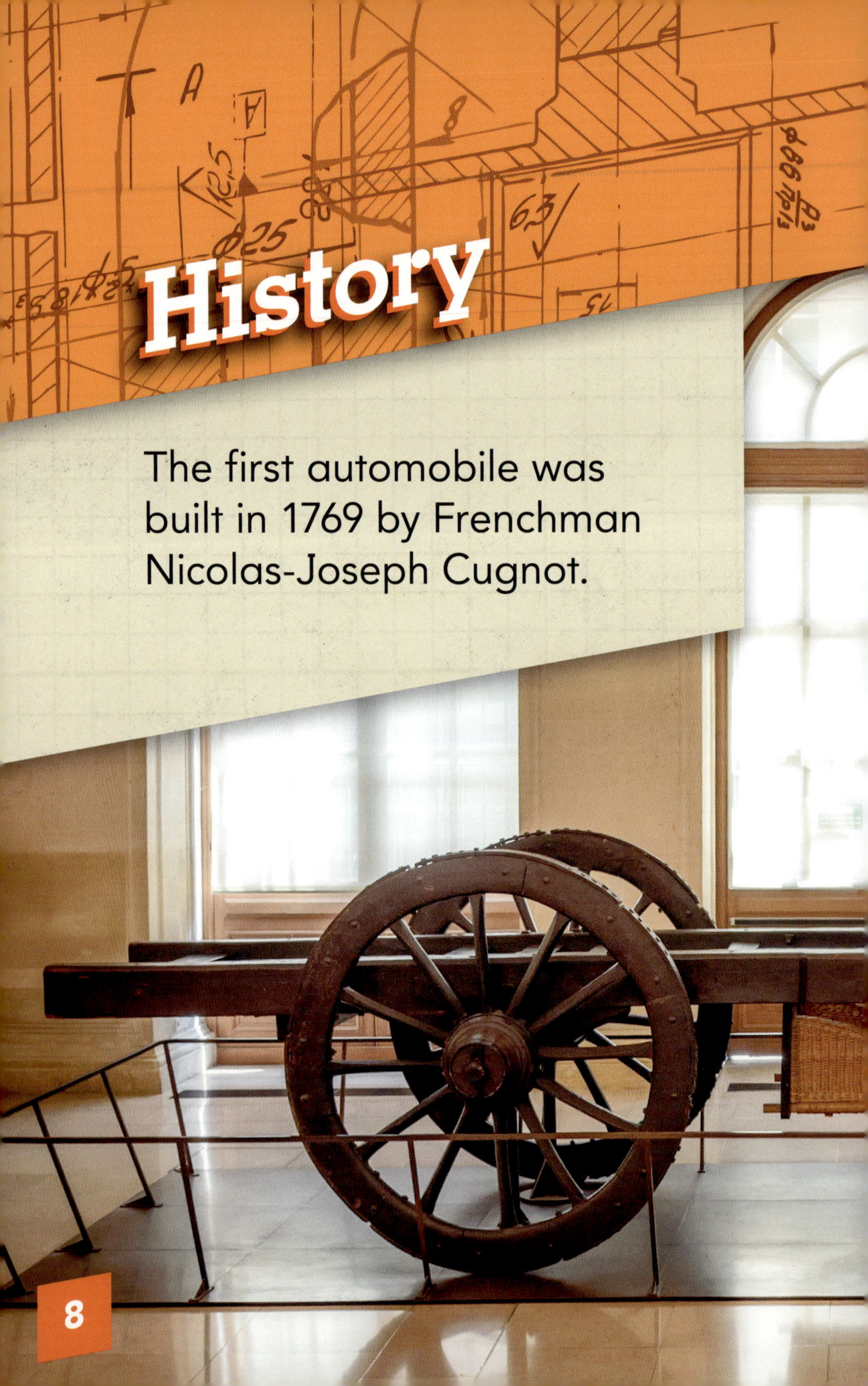

History

The first automobile was built in 1769 by Frenchman Nicolas-Joseph Cugnot.

It was powered by a **steam engine**. It traveled 2.25 miles per hour (3.6 kph).

10

Karl Benz changed automobiles forever when he built the first **practical** car in 1885. He used a four-stroke **internal combustion engine** that ran on gasoline.

Henry Ford's 1908 Model T was one of the first **mass-produced** cars. It was also the first **affordable** car. It quickly became popular around the world.

Types of Automobiles

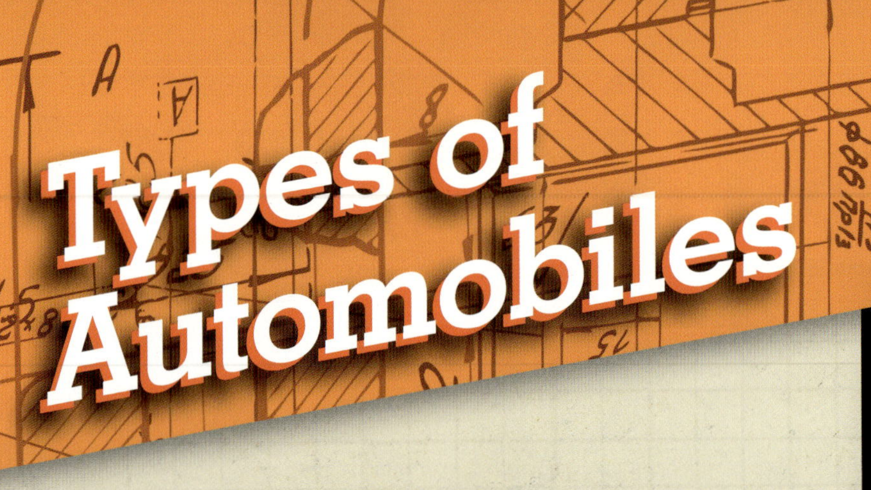

There are many types of automobiles. Most of them run on gasoline. The sedan is a four-door car that is popular for everyday use. It holds up to five passengers.

THULE

Sport-utility vehicles (SUVs) and mini-vans have a bit more space. These cars have plenty of room for passengers. They have cargo space too!

Sports cars are sleek and fast. Many have seats for just two people. Some models are designed for the top to go down. They are called **convertibles**.

Electric cars have batteries that are powered by electricity. The batteries are rechargeable.

Hybrid vehicles use both gas and electric energy to run.

More Facts

- Steering wheels went into cars in 1899. Air conditioning was added in 1939. In 1966, seat belts were routinely installed in cars.
- Today, there are more than 1.4 billion automobiles around the world!
- Most electric cars can travel 250 to 350 miles (402-563 km) on one battery charge.

Glossary

affordable – able to be obtained without spending excessive amounts of money.

convertible – a car with a top that can be folded down.

internal combustion engine – a heat engine that works by burning fuel inside itself.

mass-produced – manufactured in large quantities.

practical – able to be used; useful.

steam engine – an engine that uses steam to supply energy to its mechanical parts.

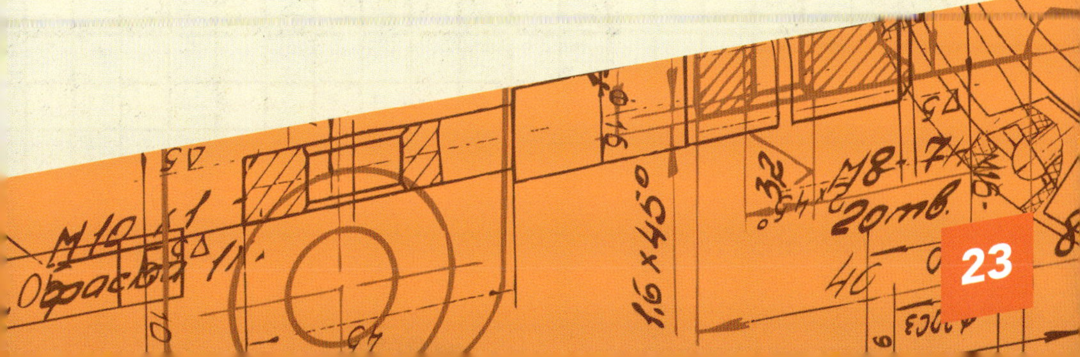

Index

Online Resources

To learn more about automobiles, please visit **abdobooklinks.com** or scan this QR code. These links are routinely monitored and updated to provide the most current information available.